This Book Belongs to:

_____
(name)

Written in:

_____
(location)

Started on:

_____
(date)

The Family Story Workbook

105 Prompts & Pointers for Collecting Your History

By Kris Spisak

DAVRO PRESS

Copyright © 2020 by Kris Spisak

ALL RIGHTS RESERVED under the Pan-American and International Copyright Conventions. This book may not be reproduced, in whole or in part, in any form or by any means electronic or mechanical, including photocopying, recording, or by any information storage and retrieval system now known or hereafter invented, without written permission from the publisher, Davro Press.

The Family Story Workbook:
105 Prompts & Pointers for Collecting Your History

ISBN: 978-1-7344524-3-3

Cover Art Credit: GAVRAN333 © 123RF.com

For further information on books from Davro Press, please visit DavroPress.com. For more information about Kris Spisak, her work, her speaking availability, and her books, please visit Kris-Spisak.com.

Contents

Why Should You Write It Down? / 7

What If You're Not A "Writer"? / 8

How Can You Use This Workbook? / 9

Generations Past / 11

All About You / 46

Remembering History / 149

Complex Conversations / 182

Language & Writing Reminders / 209

What Do You Call Your Story? / 220

Keep Sharing / 222

Author's Note / 223

Acknowledgments / 224

Why Should You Write It Down?

Once upon a time, a family changed the world, and maybe that family is yours. There are history books that tell famous tales, but there are so many more stories to be told. Why not yours? Why not now? Why not capture it for yourself and for future generations who will have questions about what life was like and where they come from? Moments both modest and monumental can so easily slip by forgotten if not recorded by someone who knows the tale.

No matter your story or your family history, there are memories to hold onto and lives to celebrate and remember. There are world-events, personal decisions made, lucky happenstances, and relationships forged in fire that shaped the present and that will reverberate into the future.

What is amazing about people is that every single one of us has a story to share. Maybe we tell them. Maybe we don't. Maybe we express them around the dinner table or at a child's bedtime. Maybe they are told in family histories or in memoirs or art or dance or poetry or recipes. Maybe we tell our stories in the traditions that we pass down from generation to generation. However we tell them, it's important that we do. Knowing where we come from adds depth to our present-day reality. Sharing how we've become who we are allows for impactful self-reflection.

Write it down because who else is going to? Write it down for you. Write it down for your family. Write it down for the historical record, whatever that means to you.

What if You're Not a "Writer"?

"Writer" is a strange word. People are so hesitant to claim it. Sure, one might "write," but to be a "writer" seems to be a more profound idea. But here's the secret: if you are putting pen to paper or digital ink to your screen, using shapes and squiggles to capture your ideas, no matter how eloquent or simple, you are a writer. Own it. It's absolutely true. You have a voice. You have opinions. You have ownership over your memories. Writers write. It's what writers do. It's your turn to begin, writer.

Storytelling is an ancient tradition. It goes back to hunts captured on cave walls and spoken tales passed down grandparent to child. The human race has always collected stories to preserve moments in time, to save them from being forgotten, to remember what it was like to live through a moment that transformed the course of people's lives. Maybe you're living through one of these moments. Write it down.

There is a time for deciding what to do with your collection of stories or perhaps for playing with the perfection of every single word, but that time doesn't have to come until later. The essential call-to-action of this workbook is to write it down. Ask questions of family and friends if that makes it easier. That doesn't make you any less of a writer. That journey of story-hunting, transcription, and capturing every single detail that you discover simply makes you an investigative reporter—diving into the story of a lifetime, your lifetime and your family members' before you.

Publishing credentials do not make a "writer." All you need is a story to tell. And you certainly have that. The right words to use shouldn't be a stumbling block. Language can be your playground. Write whatever drives you forward on a project like this. There's no race or competition here, simply a capturing of your truth, whatever that may be.

How Can You Use this Workbook?

Have you ever wanted to write down the story of your family but never known where to start?

Have you ever wanted to have a shared project between family members?

Have you ever wanted to write your memoir, but you weren't quite sure what tales of your life might be most impactful for the narrative you hope to shape?

Have you ever wanted to reflect on the moments that transformed you into the person that you are today?

This workbook is designed for all of these reasons, and more. The following pages are broken up into five sections: "Generations Past" (17 questions), "All About You" (51 questions), "Remembering History" (16 questions), "Complex Conversations" (13 questions), and "Language & Writing Reminders" (8 language-use tips).

You do not need to answer every question, nor do you have to start with number one. Write wherever your desire takes you, and if you need help, what a wonderful excuse for reaching out to family members for assistance in building the story you know is there.

We live in a miraculous age, not only for storytellers but also for story seekers. Not only do we have letters and phone calls, but we have video calls, group virtual meeting spaces, and capabilities for audio and video recording. Recognize the potential of the tools available to help you with this project and allow these tools to add even more depth to the whole.

My suggestion is to pull out a notebook and pen (or any other writing tools you may choose) for collecting your thoughts and organizing your ideas. Then return to fill the pages of this workbook once your words are ready.

No one's eyes need to see your work but your own—unless you want to share it. You get to decide. Perhaps your project will be a collection of poetry, photographs, and family tales. Perhaps it will exist in collections of music paired with snippets from your own life. Perhaps this workbook will give you the prompts for a series of video or audio interviews between you and your parents, grandparents, great-aunts, great-uncles, second cousins, and anyone else who might live far away but who is still tightly connected through family bonds and collective memories. Perhaps your effort will be one volume amidst many family story workbooks, each filled out by different individuals.

Our world is not made up of singular narratives and singular versions of the past. It is made up of all the complexities of all of our lives together. Families are as unique as skeins of yarn, and our communities are created by the weaving of these vibrant threads, each of distinctive fibers, textures, size, styles, and shades. Tell your story because that's what people do. We have since the beginning of time, and we always will. And your voice—your family's voice—is needed in this conversation.

Generations Past

When we think about telling our stories, so often we think about ourselves and our own experiences; however, that's nowhere close to the full story. We know this, yet we forget.

The following are questions for deep investigation. Perhaps you can answer many of them on your own, but maybe they are opportunities to connect with your relatives, to share stories, to ask questions, to delve deep into the people you may have always known but not on this level.

Take these questions as an opportunity to further connect, however that may be possible.

1. Let's start with a rough listing of what you know. Write down all of the names of your family members in the present day and as far back as you can go.

OPTIONS FOR DIGGING DEEPER:

- Include year and location of birth (and death) if you can.
- Include extra notes beside each name where possible (e.g., job, military experience, something he/she was known for).
- Connect with family members, if possible, to flesh this out as much as you can.

_____
_____
_____
_____
_____
_____
_____
_____
_____
_____
_____
_____
_____
_____
_____
_____
_____
_____

THE FAMILY STORY WORKBOOK: 105 PROMPTS & POINTERS FOR WRITING YOUR HISTORY

2. When you think about where your family comes from, where is that place? Or where are those places?

OPTIONS FOR DIGGING DEEPER:

- How important are these places to your family, and how does this importance show itself in daily life?
- What do you know about an old home where your family once lived? Was this your maternal or paternal side? How many details of that specific space can you share? How many people lived there? And who were they?
- Do you know of any specifics of that place (e.g., the weight of an iron key, the apple tree in the backyard, the geraniums by the front door every springtime, the front stoop where neighbors gathered, etc.)? Why do you think these details linger in family memory?

THE FAMILY STORY WORKBOOK: 105 PROMPTS & POINTERS FOR WRITING YOUR HISTORY

3. What is one of the oldest family stories that you know on your maternal side?

OPTIONS FOR DIGGING DEEPER:

- What do you know about who the involved family members were and what life was like for them at the time of this story?
- What shaped the type of people they were?
- When and where did this happen?
- Why do you think this story has been passed down amid so many others?

THE FAMILY STORY WORKBOOK: 105 PROMPTS & POINTERS FOR WRITING YOUR HISTORY 17

4. What is one of the oldest family stories that you know on your paternal side?

OPTIONS FOR DIGGING DEEPER:

- What do you know about who the involved family members were and what life was like for them at the time of this story?
- What shaped the type of people they were?
- When and where did this happen?
- Why do you think this story has been remembered?

_____
_____
_____
_____
_____
_____
_____
_____
_____
_____
_____
_____
_____
_____
_____
_____

THE FAMILY STORY WORKBOOK: 105 PROMPTS & POINTERS FOR WRITING YOUR HISTORY

5. What is a family story you've been told that you're not sure you believe?

OPTIONS FOR DIGGING DEEPER:

- What is the believable part of this story?
- What is the unbelievable part of this story?
- Why don't you believe it?
- How could it be true?
- How is the "truth" of this story perhaps not the most important part?

_____
_____
_____
_____
_____
_____
_____
_____
_____
_____
_____
_____
_____
_____
_____
_____
_____

6. What is the family story that you're proudest of—one that you want to make sure is always passed down?

OPTIONS FOR DIGGING DEEPER:

- Who were all of the people involved in this story?
- When was the first time that you heard it, and what was your reaction to it?
- What have been the reactions of others when you've retold it?
- Why is it such an essential story to hold onto?
- Do other family members have different answers to this question? If so, what stories do they recall?

THE FAMILY STORY WORKBOOK: 105 PROMPTS & POINTERS FOR WRITING YOUR HISTORY

7. Tell an old family story, from either side, that touches on the core of who your family is.

OPTIONS FOR DIGGING DEEPER:

- Who is important in this story?
- Where did it take place?
- Who first told this story to you?
- What emotion comes to mind when you think about this story? Why?

8. What is a major struggle that the maternal side of your family has had to face in the past (e.g., war, sickness, death, financial hardship, etc.), and how did your family get through?

OPTIONS FOR DIGGING DEEPER:

- How did different members of your family react to these circumstances?
- How did this struggle affect family relationships?
- What were the most difficult aspects of this moment for your family?
- What was the scariest?
- What was the most hopeful?

9. What is a major struggle that the paternal side of your family has had to face in the past (e.g., war, sickness, death, financial hardship, etc.), and how did your family get through?

OPTIONS FOR DIGGING DEEPER:

- How did different members of your family react to these circumstances?
- How did this struggle affect family relationships?
- What were the most difficult aspects of this moment for your family?
- What was the scariest?
- What was the most hopeful?

_____
_____
_____
_____
_____
_____
_____
_____
_____
_____
_____
_____
_____
_____
_____
_____

10. In the midst of one of those major struggles, how did individuals outside of the family come into the story?

OPTIONS FOR DIGGING DEEPER:

- How did others come to realize what was going on?
- How close were these individuals with the family before this struggle?
- How did this struggle change relationships?

11. What was a moment of success, accomplishment, or serendipity for your family (on either side) that changed life dramatically in some way?

OPTIONS FOR DIGGING DEEPER:

- Did this moment change things for just one individual or the whole family?
- What was different before and after this moment?
- Was the importance of this moment realized at the time or not until later?
- In the midst of this positive change in circumstances, what did no one see coming (for better or for worse)?

12. What was family life like for the different generations (and/or branches) of your family?

OPTIONS FOR DIGGING DEEPER:

- How many adults and children were there in the households?
- Describe the relationships between cousins, aunts, uncles, and other extended family members. Were they present in each other's lives? Were they not?
- What were larger family gatherings like (if applicable)?
- Were there pets or other animals important to the family?

13. What is a sibling story of your family's past—your parents or grandparents getting along with, not getting along with, or having adventures with their brother(s) and/or sister(s) as children?

OPTIONS FOR DIGGING DEEPER:

- What were the names of the siblings involved?
- What was something they discovered together?
- What was a big dispute?
- What was a moment they became closer than ever?
- If you have the opportunity to talk to anyone involved or anyone who has heard different perspectives, how do different family members remember this story differently?

_____
_____
_____
_____
_____
_____
_____
_____
_____
_____
_____
_____
_____
_____
_____

14. How did your grandparents meet?

OPTIONS FOR DIGGING DEEPER:

- Where and when did they meet?
- What were their early impressions of each other?
- How did others react to their new relationship?
- What has always struck you about their relationship story?

15. What music was special in your parents' and/or grandparents' lives?

OPTIONS FOR DIGGING DEEPER:

- What music did they enjoy?
- Where did they most commonly hear music?
- How did they most enjoy music? Did they sing? Did they dance? Did they play any instruments? And is there a moment involving any or all of these that stands out amid all others?
- What other story can you tell about your family surrounded by the music important to them?

16. How did your parents meet?

OPTIONS FOR DIGGING DEEPER:

- Where and when did they meet?
- What were their early impressions of each other?
- Do they have different versions of their meeting or early relationship story?
- What has always stayed with you about their relationship?

THE FAMILY STORY WORKBOOK: 105 PROMPTS & POINTERS FOR WRITING YOUR HISTORY

17. What did the world look like for your family before you came into it?

OPTIONS FOR DIGGING DEEPER:

- Did your family live in close proximity or were they spread far apart?
- What jobs did they hold?
- Where did they live at this time?
- What were your family's biggest concerns for the future?
- What were their biggest hopes?
- What did they take pride in more than anything else?
- What values did they live by?

All About You

Taking time out of our busy lives to pause and reflect about who we are, how we became this person, and the moments we've lived through that have made us smile, laugh, ache, cry, and dream can remind us not only where we've come from but who it is that we want to be.

Here's your chance to do more than capture your name, birthday, occupation, and address. Here's your chance to tell your story in all of its nuances. What do you want future generations to remember about who you are? Or what do you want to record and remember just for yourself?

18. What did the home(s) you grew up in look like?

OPTIONS FOR DIGGING DEEPER:

- Describe a space in a past home with all of the details that you can remember.
- Tell about the front door and what it was like to walk inside.
- What did it smell like?
- What did it sound like?
- What did it feel like when you were there?

19. Where did you sleep at night as a child?

OPTIONS FOR DIGGING DEEPER:

- Was it a bedroom that was yours alone or was it a shared space?
- Did you add anything to this space to make it feel special to you?
- If you close your eyes and imagine that place, what do you see?
- Did you have a favorite thing about this space? If so, what was it?

20. Describe the relationship you had with your siblings, cousins, or other family members.

OPTIONS FOR DIGGING DEEPER:

- Who were you closest with and why?
- Did you generally get along or was your relationship more complicated?
- Did you ever have adventures or misadventures together?
- Did you ever have to work together on something important?
- Tell a story here.

21. Do you remember a time of major division in your family? What happened to create the upset between family members?

OPTIONS FOR DIGGING DEEPER:

- When and where was this?
- Were circumstances in the larger world a part of this difficulty?
- How did this situation intensify?
- How was it resolved (if it was resolved)?

22. Did your family have a close bond with neighbors or others outside of your family in your community?

OPTIONS FOR DIGGING DEEPER:

- Who was close with your family?
- How did these bonds form?
- Who were these friends closest to in your family?
- What were their ages in relation to yours?
- What is a story you've heard (or told) countless times about these family friends?

23. Who was your closest friend when you were younger, and what was something that cemented that relationship?

OPTIONS FOR DIGGING DEEPER:

- How did you meet this friend?
- What was your first memory about them or the first thing you noticed about them?
- What was something you often did together?
- How was this friend a perfect fit for you (or not) at this time in your life?
- How was this friend's family similar to and/or different from your own?
- How did your bond with this friend impact you in some way?

_____
_____
_____
_____
_____
_____
_____
_____
_____
_____
_____
_____
_____

24. As you grew up, did your relationship with your childhood friend change? If so, how?

OPTIONS FOR DIGGING DEEPER:

- What was a moment when you were closer than ever before?
- What was a moment when the two of you were at odds?
- What was a moment when you were scared for each other?
- What was a moment when you felt like you were growing up together?

25. Was there anyone in your school or in your social circles who made life hard for you or challenged you in some way?

OPTIONS FOR DIGGING DEEPER:

- Who is the first person who comes to mind with this question, and what do you remember the most about them?
- What was the beginning of your troubles with this individual?
- What is your most painful memory associated with this person?
- Did things get worse or better from there?

_____
_____
_____
_____
_____
_____
_____
_____
_____
_____
_____
_____
_____
_____
_____
_____
_____
_____
_____

26. What foods were always present in your childhood?

OPTIONS FOR DIGGING DEEPER:

- Were any foods that your family regularly ate different from foods eaten by others in your community?
- What food is associated with the strongest memories for you?
- Describe it as if your reader has never eaten anything similar before.
- What's a specific memory involving that food?
- What emotion is most connected with that food?
- Who prepared it most often, and why?
- What was the first thing you learned how to cook? How did you learn?

_____
_____
_____
_____
_____
_____
_____
_____
_____
_____
_____
_____

27. What were your responsibilities when you were young?

OPTIONS FOR DIGGING DEEPER:

- What tasks were easiest for you, and why?
- What tasks did you try to avoid, and why?
- Was there ever a time you tried to get out of your responsibilities?
- Was there ever a time you felt like you made a true difference in the lives of your family by your actions?
- Did your tasks change as you grew up?
- Did you have any tasks or chores that would surprise a kid today?

28. What else was expected of you by your family?

OPTIONS FOR DIGGING DEEPER:

- How were these expectations communicated to you? (Verbally or otherwise?)
- Why were these expectations important to your family?
- Did you always live up to them?
- What was the hardest part about these expectations, and what would be the consequences if you fell short?

_____
_____
_____
_____
_____
_____
_____
_____
_____
_____
_____
_____
_____
_____
_____
_____
_____
_____

29. What was the most meaningful thing about your family for you as a kid?

OPTIONS FOR DIGGING DEEPER:

- What did you know was special?
- What did you appreciate?

30. What did you look forward to most about school?

OPTIONS FOR DIGGING DEEPER:

- Did you enjoy your schooling experience? Why or why not?
- Who was a teacher or other adult that made a major impression on you or taught you something important, in or out of the classroom?
- What was a moment that you spent with them that you'll always remember?

31. What was the hardest part of school for you?

OPTIONS FOR DIGGING DEEPER:

- Was it a subject taught or something else?
- What bothered you the most about this?
- How did you cope?
- What was an instance that you wished you were anywhere but in that place?

32. What were afternoons after school like for you as a kid?

OPTIONS FOR DIGGING DEEPER:

- How did you get home from school?
- Did you go straight home or somewhere else?
- Did you spend your afternoon hours with others or alone?
- What did you normally do between school and dinner?

33. What did the usual dinnertime look like for your family?

OPTIONS FOR DIGGING DEEPER:

- What did the room look like where you most commonly ate?
- Who was present? Who was not?
- Who cooked or how did the food arrive?
- Were there strict rules at your dinner table?

_____
_____
_____
_____
_____
_____
_____
_____
_____
_____
_____
_____
_____
_____
_____
_____
_____
_____
_____
_____

34. What was an article of clothing or a piece of jewelry that you once owned that you always felt good wearing?

OPTIONS FOR DIGGING DEEPER:

- How old were you when you had this item?
- Did you wear it often?
- Where did you get it?
- How could you describe it to capture exactly what it looked like and/or felt like?
- Why was it important to you?

35. When you were young, what was your favorite thing to do by yourself?

OPTIONS FOR DIGGING DEEPER:

- When did you do this?
- Where did you do this?
- What was it about this activity that you enjoyed so much or that you found solace in?

36. When you were young, what was your favorite thing to do with friends?

OPTIONS FOR DIGGING DEEPER:

- Who was usually involved?
- What was the first time you all did this together?
- What were the unspoken traditions of this activity?
- What is your favorite memory centered around this activity?

_____
_____
_____
_____
_____
_____
_____
_____
_____
_____
_____
_____
_____
_____
_____
_____
_____
_____
_____

37. When you were growing up, did you ever wish that your family was different? How so?

OPTIONS FOR DIGGING DEEPER:

- Did you feel like your parents were protecting you or that you were protecting your parents?
- Who did you feel like you needed to protect most in your family? Why?
- Was it easy to talk to your parents about your life?
- Who did you feel most safe with in your family? Why?

38. When you think about the people who raised you, what words come to mind that embody who they are/were? Can you narrow it down to just five words each?

OPTIONS FOR DIGGING DEEPER:

- What was your mother, father, and/or any other parental figure really good at that not everyone knows?
- What guiding principles were important to them as they raised you?
- How has your understanding of your parents changed over time?

39. What is something you learned from your father or another close man in your life?

OPTIONS FOR DIGGING DEEPER:

- Did you learn this lesson by him actively teaching you or by coming to an understanding about it after observing him?
- How did this lesson impact you?
- Have you ever taught this same lesson to someone else? How did you teach it?

40. What is something you learned from your mother or another close woman in your life?

OPTIONS FOR DIGGING DEEPER:

- Did you learn this lesson by her actively teaching you or by coming to an understanding about it after observing her?
- How did this lesson impact you?
- Have you ever taught this same lesson to someone else? How did you teach it?

41. What is something you remember learning from one of your grandparents or an older member of your family circle?

OPTIONS FOR DIGGING DEEPER:

- How did they teach you?
- Where did they teach you?
- What was it about this lesson that stuck with you the most?

_____
_____
_____
_____
_____
_____
_____
_____
_____
_____
_____
_____
_____
_____
_____
_____
_____
_____
_____

42. What is something that happened to you that you never told your parents?

OPTIONS FOR DIGGING DEEPER:

- Where were you?
- Who were you with?
- How did you get into this circumstance?
- How were you feeling in this moment?
- Why did you never tell?

_____
_____
_____
_____
_____
_____
_____
_____
_____
_____
_____
_____
_____
_____
_____
_____
_____
_____
_____
_____

43. What was the first time you ever made money?

OPTIONS FOR DIGGING DEEPER:

- How old were you?
- How did you get this job, or how did you set up this business?
- Did anyone help you?
- Why was making money and undertaking this effort important to you at this time?
- Did you have a plan for your money earned?

44. What was something you've seen in your life that you probably weren't supposed to see?

OPTIONS FOR DIGGING DEEPER:

- How old were you?
- Where were you?
- Did anyone else know you were there?
- What emotions were you experiencing in that moment?
- Did you ever talk to anyone about this?

45. What was your favorite thing to learn about when you were younger, and why?

OPTIONS FOR DIGGING DEEPER:

- How did you become interested in this topic?
- If it was a subject in school, was there a particular person who made this topic interesting to you?
- How did you explore this topic on your own?
- What was it about this subject that was so fascinating to you?

46. What did your summer look like as a kid?

OPTIONS FOR DIGGING DEEPER:

- Did you have a job?
- What were others' expectations of you?
- Who did you spend your time with?
- What is your favorite outdoor memory of a past summertime?

47. What did you want to be when you grew up?

OPTIONS FOR DIGGING DEEPER:

- When did you first have this idea?
- What sparked it?
- Did your "dream job" evolve into other ideas as you grew up?
- What passions did you dream of pursuing?
- When you imagined yourself as a "grown-up," what did you see?

_____
_____
_____
_____
_____
_____
_____
_____
_____
_____
_____
_____
_____
_____
_____
_____
_____
_____
_____

48. When you were younger, what was some of your favorite music?

OPTIONS FOR DIGGING DEEPER:

- What is a story of your life connected to a specific musician's or band's music?
- If you were going to buy music to listen to, where would you go? What did that place look like, feel like, and sound like? What would your purchase look like?
- Is there a song that you hear today and it brings you right back into one specific moment? What is that song, and what is that moment?
- Did you ever see a live music show? What was your first? What was your favorite?

49. What is your favorite holiday, and what makes it so special for you?

OPTIONS FOR DIGGING DEEPER:

- Is your answer the same now as when you were younger?
- What's a favorite memory from that holiday?
- What has changed about your favorite holiday between your youth and now?
- What traditions did you and do you have around this holiday?

50. What did you take a lot of pride in about yourself when you were young?

OPTIONS FOR DIGGING DEEPER:

- What was an area where you excelled or something where you knew you were special?
- Was this a secret pride, or did others see you excel?
- What was a moment when you felt really good about who you were during that time of your life?

51. What's a story from your youth when you made the wrong choice?

OPTIONS FOR DIGGING DEEPER:

- What were your motivations?
- What did you think would happen?
- What went wrong?
- Did you know it was wrong before you did it?
- Would you make a different choice if you could go back and do it again?

52. What's a secret that you've kept?

OPTIONS FOR DIGGING DEEPER:

- Why was it important for you to keep this secret?
- Who did you keep it for? Yourself? Someone else?
- Who else knew?
- How well did you keep this secret?

53. What was a moment in your life when you were truly scared?

OPTIONS FOR DIGGING DEEPER:

- Where were you?
- Who were you with?
- How did this moment come to be?
- Write down every emotion of that moment you can think of.
- Capture every sight, sound, smell, and feeling you can remember.

54. What was one of the happiest moments in your life? (Marriage and birth stories will come later, so don't pick one of those if they apply here.)

OPTIONS FOR DIGGING DEEPER:

- Was this happiness a surprise, or was it something you worked for or saw coming?
- Who was with you?
- Where were you?
- What are the pieces of this story that you'll never forget?
- How did that moment affect the rest of your life (in a big or small way)?

55. When did you consider yourself a "grown-up"?

OPTIONS FOR DIGGING DEEPER:

- Was this a shift that happened to you internally or externally (i.e., did you feel the shift in yourself or did you assume your new role because that was the expectation)?
- What was one of the first specific moments when you knew you were an adult?
- How did you handle it?
- What did you learn from this moment?

56. If you've been married, what do you remember about your wedding day? (Be sure to include the date and location.)

OPTIONS FOR DIGGING DEEPER:

- What are the moments of that day that stick in your mind more than any others?
- What was something about that day that was unexpected?
- What sights, sounds, smells, tastes, or feelings about that day are still vivid for you?

_____
_____
_____
_____
_____
_____
_____
_____
_____
_____
_____
_____
_____
_____
_____
_____
_____

57. If you are a parent, what do you remember about the time between knowing a child was expected and the due date?

OPTIONS FOR DIGGING DEEPER:

- When and/or how did you learn that your family was about to grow?
- What were your feelings during this time?
- What do you remember about your internal and/or external preparations?

58. What are the first memories you have of your child(ren)?

OPTIONS FOR DIGGING DEEPER:

- What was the first thing you noticed about your child(ren)?
- What emotions did you feel in that moment?
- What did you hope for most in that moment?
- What about that moment in your life stands out in your memory more than anything else?

_____
_____
_____
_____
_____
_____
_____
_____
_____
_____
_____
_____
_____
_____
_____
_____
_____
_____
_____
_____

59. How has having children redefined or reshaped who you are? (if applicable)

OPTIONS FOR DIGGING DEEPER:

- What was the first moment when you felt that this shift was true for you? Was it a matter of new responsibility or something one of your children did or said?
- What was a situation when you know you behaved differently because you were with your child(ren)?

60. How did gaining a niece, nephew, godchild, grandchild, or other new family member shift your life in some way? (if applicable)

OPTIONS FOR DIGGING DEEPER:

- How was your role different from being a parent?
- What was a time when you fully embraced your new role?
- Did this role have any challenges for you?
- What have been your favorite parts (so far) of having a relationship with your young family member(s)?

_____
_____
_____
_____
_____
_____
_____
_____
_____
_____
_____
_____
_____
_____
_____
_____
_____
_____
_____
_____

61. Have you ever gained, lost, or shifted a job in a way that was life-changing for you?

OPTIONS FOR DIGGING DEEPER:

- What were the circumstances before this change?
- How and why did this job change occur?
- Why was this shift so dramatic for you at this time in your life?
- What do you remember most about this moment?

62. What was a moment in your adult life that shifted your understanding of something important?

OPTIONS FOR DIGGING DEEPER:

- What specifically about that moment evoked this change in your thoughts?
- Was it something someone taught you, something observed, or something else?
- Were you alone or with others? If with others, did they realize the impact of the moment as well?
- Why do you think this memory has stayed with you?

63. What was the most difficult lesson you've ever had to learn? How did you learn it?

OPTIONS FOR DIGGING DEEPER:

- Was it a lesson learned in a moment or a lesson learned over a longer amount of time?
- Was anyone else involved in teaching you this?
- How much work did you have to put in to learn it?
- What shifted inside of you with this lesson?

_____
_____
_____
_____
_____
_____
_____
_____
_____
_____
_____
_____
_____
_____
_____
_____
_____
_____

64. How does your family's cultural heritage affect how you see the world?

OPTIONS FOR DIGGING DEEPER:

- What regions and/or countries have been home for your family?
- What languages have been part of your family experience?
- What traditions are a core piece of your family?
- How do any of these details affect your belief system or sense of self?
- How might different family members answer this differently?

65. What are the guiding ideas of your life that define who you are?

OPTIONS FOR DIGGING DEEPER:

- Pick five words that you feel describe you best, or alternatively, five words that you want to describe you best.
- How have important values of your life shifted between how you see yourself (and what is important) today versus how you might have seen yourself (and what was important) when you were younger?
- What is a moment of your life when you felt so absolutely yourself, living the life and being the person that you knew you could be?
- Do you think others would define you by these or similar words? Why or why not?

66. What is something that you've always wanted to do but haven't (yet)?

OPTIONS FOR DIGGING DEEPER:

- What inspired your interest in this?
- How do you imagine it?
- Have you shared this dream with anyone? If so, who, and what was their reaction?
- Do you ever plan to do it?

67. Where is a place that you've always wanted to go but have never been? What is it about this place that intrigues you?

OPTIONS FOR DIGGING DEEPER:

- What inspired your interest in this place?
- How do you imagine it?
- What would be your ideal day there?
- Do you ever plan to go?

68. What is a moment in your life (not yet mentioned in these pages) that impacted you and transformed you into the person that you are today?

OPTIONS FOR DIGGING DEEPER:

- When and where was this?
- Who was with you?
- Did this transformation happen suddenly in that moment or over time?

Remembering History

There are times in our lives that we'll always remember, not just for the date but for where we were exactly in the moment that something world-changing happened. Sometimes, these occasions are personal. Sometimes, they are global.

We cannot take these memories for granted, nor can we let them be lost because we never took the time to record them. Perhaps this is the moment to make history in a new way by writing it all down, for that in itself is momentous and worth celebrating.

69. What do you remember about the 1963 March on Washington, Martin Luther King, Jr.'s words, and/or King's 1968 assassination? (if applicable)

OPTIONS FOR DIGGING DEEPER:

- How old were you?
- How aware were you of Martin Luther King, Jr. and his work?
- How did you feel the impact of these moments?
- How did the people around you?
- Describe a memory of these times.
- Ask a family member to share their memories.

_____
_____
_____
_____
_____
_____
_____
_____
_____
_____
_____
_____
_____
_____
_____
_____
_____

THE FAMILY STORY WORKBOOK: 105 PROMPTS & POINTERS FOR WRITING YOUR HISTORY

70. What do you remember about the deaths of John F. Kennedy and Bobby Kennedy? (if applicable)

OPTIONS FOR DIGGING DEEPER:

- How old were you?
- How did you learn about these assassinations?
- What was the reaction of those around you?
- What was yours?
- How did these moments impact the world around you?

THE FAMILY STORY WORKBOOK: 105 PROMPTS & POINTERS FOR WRITING YOUR HISTORY

71. What do you remember about the moon landing? (if applicable)

OPTIONS FOR DIGGING DEEPER:

- How old were you?
- Did you watch it live?
- What were the reactions of the people in the room with you?
- What was yours?
- How did conversations continue about this event after it happened?

THE FAMILY STORY WORKBOOK: 105 PROMPTS & POINTERS FOR WRITING YOUR HISTORY

72. What do you remember about the end of the Vietnam War? (if applicable)

OPTIONS FOR DIGGING DEEPER:

- How old were you?
- What were your thoughts about this war?
- Or about war in general?
- How did you learn what you knew about the Vietnam War?
- What did its end mean to you?
- How has time shaped your perspective of this era?

THE FAMILY STORY WORKBOOK: 105 PROMPTS & POINTERS FOR WRITING YOUR HISTORY

73. What do you remember about the U.S. Bicentennial (1976)? (if applicable)

OPTIONS FOR DIGGING DEEPER:

- How old were you?
- What was the spirit of this moment?
- How did you celebrate or see others celebrate?
- What memory still lives in your mind from this occasion?

74. Where were you when the Challenger exploded? (if applicable)

OPTIONS FOR DIGGING DEEPER:

- How old were you?
- Did you watch it live?
- What was the reaction of the people in the room with you?
- What was yours?

THE FAMILY STORY WORKBOOK: 105 PROMPTS & POINTERS FOR WRITING YOUR HISTORY

75. What do you remember about the Berlin Wall coming down? (if applicable)

OPTIONS FOR DIGGING DEEPER:

- What was the significance of this moment to you?
- What images from television or other media stay in your mind?
- How had you learned about the Berlin Wall and what it meant?
- Did anyone around you have strong opinions about this moment?
- Has your understanding of importance of this wall coming down evolved over time?

THE FAMILY STORY WORKBOOK: 105 PROMPTS & POINTERS FOR WRITING YOUR HISTORY

76. How has watching television and/or movies changed since you were younger?

OPTIONS FOR DIGGING DEEPER:

- Describe the first television set that you remember and what you watched on it.
- What were changes in television technology that wowed you (e.g. color television, remote controls, cable, television size, etc.)?
- What's a childhood memory of going to the movie theater? What did you see? What was the experience in the theater like?
- What was a movie that you loved when you saw it? Why?
- What was a more recent movie that you've seen in a movie theater? What was the experience in the theater like?
- What devices have you owned for watching movies in your own home (e.g., VCRs, DVD players, etc.)? Do you remember your reactions to any of this technology when it was new?
- How do you most commonly watch television/movies today?

THE FAMILY STORY WORKBOOK: 105 PROMPTS & POINTERS FOR WRITING YOUR HISTORY

77. How have cars and car travel changed during your lifetime?

OPTIONS FOR DIGGING DEEPER:

- Did you ever have a favorite car or one that has always lingered in your memory?
- What was so special about that vehicle?
- Was this a vehicle you owned or one you only dreamed of owning?
- When you think about a road trip, is there one specific journey of yours that comes to mind? If so, what vehicle did you travel in for that trip?
- What changes have you seen in cars over the years that impacted the way you experience cars (as a passenger or as a driver)?

THE FAMILY STORY WORKBOOK: 105 PROMPTS & POINTERS FOR WRITING YOUR HISTORY

78. How has your usage of phones changed in your lifetime?

OPTIONS FOR DIGGING DEEPER:

- What do you remember about making phone calls when you were young?
- How did this change for you and your family over the years?
- What are the first images from pop culture that you remember in regard to early mobile phones and/or their possibilities?
- What do you remember about the first time you saw or used a mobile phone?
- How has your mobile phone usage evolved?

79. What are your earliest memories of the internet and the world wide web?

OPTIONS FOR DIGGING DEEPER:

- Where did you first have access to the internet?
- How did you first explore or use the world wide web?
- What was the most fascinating part about it to you?
- What was the most mind-blowing?
- How has your usage and the world's usage of the internet changed between the 1990s and today?

THE FAMILY STORY WORKBOOK: 105 PROMPTS & POINTERS FOR WRITING YOUR HISTORY

80. What do you remember about "Y2K"?

OPTIONS FOR DIGGING DEEPER:

- Where were you on New Year's Eve that year (December 31, 1999)?
- Who were you with?
- Were you (or anyone you knew) nervous about what might happen when the calendar changed from 1999 to 2000?
- What had the media told you might happen?
- What did ringing in the year 2000 feel like for you?

THE FAMILY STORY WORKBOOK: 105 PROMPTS & POINTERS FOR WRITING YOUR HISTORY

81. Where were you on 9/11?

OPTIONS FOR DIGGING DEEPER:

- How did you learn about what was happening?
- Who did you spend time with or talk to on that day?
- What were your emotions like?
- How did your view of your world and the world at large shift? Or did it?

THE FAMILY STORY WORKBOOK: 105 PROMPTS & POINTERS FOR WRITING YOUR HISTORY

82. What were your earliest thoughts on social media?

OPTIONS FOR DIGGING DEEPER:

- When did you receive your first social media account invitation or when did you first explore what this meant?
- Why did you open that first social media account? Or why did you choose not to?
- What was your first social media account and how did you use it? (if any)
- Are you still active on social media platforms? If so, which one(s)?
- How have your thoughts and behaviors changed in regard to social media over the years?

THE FAMILY STORY WORKBOOK: 105 PROMPTS & POINTERS FOR WRITING YOUR HISTORY

83. What will you always remember about 2020?

OPTIONS FOR DIGGING DEEPER:

- What were your thoughts when you first started hearing about COVID-19? Did these thoughts evolve over the weeks and months that passed? What sparked these changed ideas?
- What were your thoughts on the Black Lives Matter movement prior to the spring of 2020? Did these thoughts change or evolve for you in the spring of 2020? What about as time moved on?
- What were your thoughts as the SpaceX shuttle, the first privately-owned, manned shuttle took off for its maiden voyage?
- Did virtual schooling and the necessity to rethink education during this time have an effect on your household? How so?
- Did the political divisions of 2020 affect you or any of your relationships?
- How did visits with your family or time with those in your household change during this time?
- What were the biggest emotions you felt during this year?

THE FAMILY STORY WORKBOOK: 105 PROMPTS & POINTERS FOR WRITING YOUR HISTORY

84. What is something your generation lived through that you wish more people knew or talked about?

OPTIONS FOR DIGGING DEEPER:

- Why is this so important to you?
- Why don't you think more people know or talk about this?
- Why do you think it is essential that more people are aware of it?

THE FAMILY STORY WORKBOOK: 105 PROMPTS & POINTERS FOR WRITING YOUR HISTORY

Complex Conversations

Before you reach the end of this workbook, seize the opportunity to not just recall your life's moments but also your life's ideas.

There are no right or wrong answers to the following questions. Writing down your beliefs simply allows a chance to more fully flesh out who you are, who you have been, and who you want to be. The philosophical does not have to be left to the philosophers. Your voice can be equally profound, if you dare to use it.

85. What does "family" mean to you?

OPTIONS FOR DIGGING DEEPER:

- Define this term as if you were giving a definition to your great-great-grandchildren. What would you want them to know about what family meant in your eyes?
- Has the importance of family changed for you over time?
- How have age, proximity, and/or distance shifted your appreciation for the people in your life?
- What was a moment in your life when you realized how unique family relationships are amid all of the other relationships in your life?
- How has being a member of your family impacted you?

_____
_____
_____
_____
_____
_____
_____
_____
_____
_____
_____
_____

86. What does "faith" mean to you?

OPTIONS FOR DIGGING DEEPER:

- What is an early memory of when you began to understand the idea of faith?
- How has this concept changed for you over time?
- Do you believe that the idea of "faith" has changed in the world over your lifetime?
- When you think about words like "faith," "religion," and "spirituality," what stands out most in your mind?
- What was a moment in your life when faith was critical and/or poignant for you?

87. What does "success" mean to you?

OPTIONS FOR DIGGING DEEPER:

- When you were a kid and imagined a "successful life," what did that look like to you?
- How has this changed for you over time?
- How has this changed in the world over your lifetime?
- What was a moment in your life when success or failure seemed imminent, and the difference mattered intensely to you?
- Have you ever had to make a decision or take action in your life that affected your success, however you've defined it, in a dramatic way?

88. What does "equality" mean to you?

OPTIONS FOR DIGGING DEEPER:

- Has this definition changed for you over time?
- Was there a particular moment in your life when the idea of "equality" become more significant than ever before?
- Was there a moment in your life that shifted your understanding of this concept?
- Has this changed in the world over your lifetime?

89. What does "fairness" mean to you?

OPTIONS FOR DIGGING DEEPER:

- What was a time in your early years when something seemed incredibly unfair to you?
- Has your definition of "fairness" changed for you over time? If so, how and why?
- Has this changed in the world over your lifetime? Why do you answer the way that you do?
- Is all fair in love and war?

90. What does "respect" mean to you?

OPTIONS FOR DIGGING DEEPER:

- How were you taught the meaning of this word?
- How do people demonstrate their understanding of this word?
- How has the definition of this word changed over the course of time, either for you personally or for the greater world in your opinion?
- What is most important to you concerning ideas of respect?

91. What does "happiness" mean to you?

OPTIONS FOR DIGGING DEEPER:

- When you were younger and you thought about living a happy life, what came to mind for you?
- Has this changed for you over time?
- Has this changed in the world or in the culture surrounding you over your lifetime?
- Why is happiness or the pursuit of happiness important to you (or is it)?
- What was a moment in your life when you were at your happiest?
- What do you wish you were told about happiness?

92. What does "living a good life" mean to you?

OPTIONS FOR DIGGING DEEPER:

- How do ideas of "family," "faith," "success," "equality," "fairness," "respect" and "happiness" play into this definition? Are there other core ideas that are important to you in this definition?
- How has this changed for you over time?
- How has this changed in the world over your lifetime?
- Or in your country?
- What is a story of your own life where you have understood what "living a good life" can look like?

_____
_____
_____
_____
_____
_____
_____
_____
_____
_____
_____
_____
_____
_____
_____
_____
_____
_____

93. How do you feel you've had or not had a voice in your lifetime?

OPTIONS FOR DIGGING DEEPER:

- How has this been true or not within your household, within your community, or within your nation?
- Is your answer different between the past and the present?
- What has or hasn't changed?

94. In what ways has the world (your household, your community, your region, your country, etc.) become more or less accepting of others during your lifetime?

OPTIONS FOR DIGGING DEEPER:

- How has this changed for you personally over time?
- How have you ever felt different?
- What was a moment in your life when someone else's difference was at the core of the moment? How did you react? How did others?
- What are your opinions on the words "tolerance," "inclusion," and "diversity"?

95. Do you think the role of being a "mom" or "dad" or parent in general has changed since you were a kid?

OPTIONS FOR DIGGING DEEPER:

- How did your grandparents understand these rolls?
- How did your parents?
- What is different about the world today when it comes to parenting?
- Tell a story from your life that demonstrates these differences.

_____
_____
_____
_____
_____
_____
_____
_____
_____
_____
_____
_____
_____
_____
_____
_____
_____
_____
_____
_____
_____

96. What are your hopes for the future?

OPTIONS FOR DIGGING DEEPER:

- What are your hopes for the future of your family, your country, and/or the world?
- What is something you wish for future generations that you do not have or that you feel could be better?
- What do you hope will remain the same?

97. The only constant in life, as they say, is change. What about the English language itself? What are your feelings about the evolution of words, language, grammar rules, and communications as a whole?

OPTIONS FOR DIGGING DEEPER:

- How important is it to have a grip on your grammar?
- Do you have a language pet peeve or an annoyance about those who care dramatically about English language rules?
- What is your favorite word?
- What is your favorite expression?
- Are their regionalisms that you commonly use that someone who doesn't live near you might not understand?
- What do you say frequently, something that others might associate with you specifically?
- If you get the final word and final punctuation mark in this workbook, what is it that you still want to say?

_____
_____
_____
_____
_____
_____
_____
_____
_____
_____
_____

Language & Writing Reminders

Our voices should never be silenced or slowed for fear of mistakes in the initial phase of writing. However, after you're all finished, if you plan on bringing notes you have taken into a final form in this workbook or if you plan on taking your story out of this workbook and into another larger narrative—from a comprehensive family history to a memoir to a fictionalized story or whatever it might be—this is where editing becomes important.

Yes, I just said the "editing" word, and I felt you cringe. Deep breath, everyone. Remember, editing isn't about tearing things apart. Editing is lifting up a work, polishing it until it shines. The moment we decide to share ideas that trickled out of our minds and into written words is the moment we need to begin making our ideas as clear as possible. You've got it, writers. And yes, I'm officially calling you a "writer" now, whether you would like to accept the title or not.

What follows here are writing tips from my ever-growing online collection that can help your cause when considering storytelling from your past and about your family. But remember, correct language usage isn't just a matter of rules. Sometimes, it's a hunt, a quest, a matter of discovery. And sometimes, language simply evolves.

It grows up. Just like people.

The best we can do is to try to get it right.

98. "Eldest" vs. "Oldest"

YOU KNOW YOU'VE WONDERED about this. What on earth is the difference between "oldest" and "eldest"? Don't they mean the same thing? Is this a ye old colonial spelling—like "ye" instead of "the"—that for some grammar-forsaken reason refuses to fade into the linguistic history books?

The answer is simpler than you realize: **"oldest" and "eldest" do indeed have the same definition. The only difference is that "eldest" is used when referring to family relationships.** Do you have to use "eldest" in these situations? Of course not. There's no grammarian coup over this distinction. However, it does explain why the word "eldest" brings to mind the Bennett sisters from *Pride and Prejudice* and Louisa May Alcott's *Little Women*. It's all about family relationships.

I don't know if birth order has anything to do with grammar persnicketiness. Do eldest children have a tendency to dot their i's and cross their t's? Are youngest children inclined toward utter grammar rebellion? That first known person to drop an "OMG" in 1917—yep, I said that date correctly, 1917—was he a youngest child? I bet he was.

Here's what I do know:

- Lindley Murray, often called the "Father of Grammar" was an eldest child.
- Noah Webster, American English renegade, was the 4th child out of 5.
- Ben Franklin, English language revolutionary among so much else, was the 15th child out of 17. (Yikes, power to that mama ...)

So whether you are the eldest sibling or the youngest, you finally have your answer. Though, is anyone else bummed there isn't some equally antiquated variation of "youngest" to match? Just me? I don't believe it.

99. "Great-greats" and the Hyphens Surrounding Them

FAMILY TREES CAN BE complicated, but you know what shouldn't be complicated? The lines and hyphens that make up the branches. Yet time and time again, we are baffled by simple punctuation marks. We can conquer punctuation once and for all—at least when it comes to our great-grandparents and our great grandparents. Both can be correct usages, but do you know the difference?

Here's your hint: can't grandparents be absolutely great to their grandchildren?

If you're saying, sure, then it's because these are "great grandparents." They're lovely. They're awesome. They're wonderful. In this case, "great" is just a descriptor of these dedicated grandparents.

However, **if your "great-grandparents," as in the parents of your grand-parents, are the subject of the conversation, a hyphen is needed.** The same is true for great-aunts, great-uncles, great-great-great-grandparents, and anyone else who falls into a category where "great" is not just a kind adjective but a generational distancer.

You might see the occasional comma used in these cases, but you can be savvier than that. The correct punctuation for your family tree is "great-grandparents." The correct punctuation for their parents would be your "great-great-grandparents." And their parents would be your "great-great-great-grandparents," and on and on.

Hyphens aren't out to intimidate. They're out to clarify all of that greatness. And what's not great about that?

100. "I Couldn't Be Prouder" or "I Couldn't Be More Proud"

IF YOUR MOM HAS EVER told you she couldn't be more proud, maybe she said it because it was true. But before you start feeling all the warm fuzzies, maybe it was just a matter of linguistics. "More proud" isn't really a thing. She couldn't be "more proud," because that combination of words isn't technically correct.

I feel like I might have just broken some hearts. Don't worry. I'm sure your mom couldn't be prouder of you. That's the correct form of the sentiment.

When it comes to "superlatives" (ooh, grammar jargon, sorry it slipped in), sometimes it's tricky when deciding which words get "-er" or "-est" endings and which words get "more" or "most" placed in front of them. As with most things in the English language, there's an easy rule for knowing the difference; unsurprisingly, there are also a lot of exceptions to the easy rule—but we'll worry about that later.

- Superlative rule #1 – If the adjective you're using has one syllable, use the "-er" and "-est" suffixes (e.g., "proud," "prouder," "proudest"; "high," "higher," "highest"; or "thick," "thicker," "thickest").
- Superlative rule #2 – If the adjective you're using has three or more syllables, always use "more" or "most" in front of the word (e.g., "terrified," "more terrified," "most terrified"; "intelligent," "more intelligent," "most intelligent"; "confusing," "more confusing," "most confusing").

You'll notice a major gap in these rules, and I bet you can already think of a few exceptions. But what about the two syllable words? I hear you. What about fun, "more fun," and "most fun"? And what about "good," "better," "best"?

I know, I know ... the English language is one of rebellion. However, knowing the rule in the first place gives you a good start. (If it helps, for those two-syllable adjectives, there is a secondary rule concerning the final letters of the word, which is mostly followed.)

To get back to the original debate, "proud" is one syllable. Thus, **"prouder" is the correct form.**

You don't have to correct your mom, but if you're saying it to your own kids—or dogs or peacocks—make sure you get it right.

101. "Naval Gazing" vs. "Navel-Gazing"

IF YOU'RE DOING LOTS of "naval-gazing," maybe you're missing a sailor or maybe you're a spy. But I'm guessing it might be a typo if you're writing about excessive introspection.

"Navel-gazing," meaning the contemplation of your own thoughts, concerns, and existence (often to a self-absorbed degree), was first used in 1959, but oh, how the spelling confusion has lingered since then.

I recommend being careful with this word that slants toward the egotistical and making sure you understand what it often implies. It definitely shouldn't imply anything about shipping vessels, submarines, or U.S. Navy ports of call. The good news is that this typo isn't one based in solipsism, but the bad news is that it doesn't reflect well on you. A little more contemplation is needed here, actually.

And speaking of contemplation, if you're using the idea in terms of meditation, the literal gazing upon one's navel, there's always the alternate term "omphaloskepsis," literally *omphalos* (navel) + *skepsis* (the act of looking) in Greek, which is practiced by Eastern mystics; however, this isn't the most common use of "navel-gazing" today.

Navel oranges also shouldn't be a part of this conversation, but we all have our ways of remembering certain phrases. If visualizing yourself in the produce section of the grocery store helps get this right, that can work too.

102. "Now a Days" vs. "Nowadays" vs. "Nowdays"

SOMETIMES, WHEN IT comes to spelling, we might feel like we're in a daze, especially when it comes to words that we hear said more than we see written. If you were writing this phrase in the fourteenth century—if you were lucky enough to know how to read or write in that era—you would have used the multiple-word form, but language has evolved since then.

Nowadays, the correct spelling is "nowadays"—yes, all one word. No hyphens or spaces needed.

People seem to get nervous around words like this, as if they're just sticking things together that don't really belong, portmanteaus like "baconator" or "sharknado." But like "spork" and "netiquette," "nowadays" is a mashup that truly works.

"Nowdays," on the other hand, is simply a typo. I feel like I have days like that sometimes, when everyone seems to want things now, now, now ... but that's not really what anyone's going for with this attempt at spelling.

103. "Pastime" vs. "Past time"

PERHAPS YOU COULD SAY that it's "past time" that we understood the difference between "pastime" and "past time." Perhaps you could say that closely examining language, storytelling, and how we use our words to empower us all is my favorite "pastime." Do you see the difference in these two spellings?

Remember:

- "Past time," as two words, is often written in a sentence like "It's past time that …" It's a reference to something being overdue, to something that should have happened already. "Past time" could also simply be a reference to a "time" in the "past," as in something historical.
- **"Pastime" is a noun, meaning something that one might do regularly in their free time.**
- "To pass time" is, of course, different still—because the English language likes to keep you on your toes. **"To pass time" means to spend time doing something, anything, while time goes by.**

The word "pastime," as in that hobby, comes from the squishing together of "pass" and "time," not a squishing together of "past" and "time." Sure "squishing together" isn't the technical phrase. You can see where the same transformation happened in words like "nowadays" and "troubleshoot." We could talk truncation or near-portmanteaus, but I feel you falling asleep just as I'm jotting down this very sentence. As always, knowing the jargon is far less important than knowing how to use language properly.

"Pastime" has been used since the 15th century, and I can only imagine how pastimes have changed since that time. So much in the world has changed since then. So much is still changing day by day in our present reality. It's true with grammar, and it's true with so much else, isn't it?

104. "Right" vs. "Rite" of Passage

DISCUSSIONS OF "RIGHTS" are sometimes tricky. Discussions of "Rites" are often equally complicated. Discussions of why I could choose to capitalize both of those words might be intimidating. But discussing the differences between "rights" and "rites" shouldn't be a matter that mystifies us.

Remember:

- "Right" can mean correct; it can mean the opposite of left. It can also mean what is just, fair, and proper, or the embodiment of something that you can claim as your due.
- "Rite" is often (but not always) used in a religious sense, as a ceremonial act or initiation that one goes through.

Once these definitions are sorted out, we can tackle the question of a "Right" or "Rite" of Passage.

- **A "Rite of Passage" is a moment or ritual that acts as a crossover to a new stage of life.** A religious confirmation is a rite of passage; a graduation is too; you could argue the survival of middle school is a rite of passage in many people's lives. This is a phrase that was first used in 1909, but I'm guessing it wasn't because of that last example. Let's all take a deep breath and move past the memory of that last example.
- A "Right of Passage" doesn't come up nearly as much as the first. It could refer to the ability or permission to cross through a certain territory. In fantasy writing, it might include trolls that are blocking a bridge. Or, in other writing, it might be a typo.

Yes, you can get this right. Correct language use is not a rite of passage—the understanding of "moot" vs. "mute" or "hone" vs. "home" as a gateway to adulthood?—but maybe it should be. Or is this going too far?

105. "Succession" vs. "Secession"

WHETHER YOU'RE CREATING your succession plan or your secession plan, it's good to think it through—yes, even with your spelling. Even the best of ideas can fall through without the right attention to detail. Maybe you've learned that the hard way. Maybe you've learned it by a typo hitting you in the face. (This is absolutely one that can do that.)

Remember:

- **"Succession" is the order in line for a leadership position or simply the process of following in order.** We're talking heirs to the throne, groomed employees, or ketchup bottles on a conveyor belt. (You didn't see that last example coming did you?) "Succession" is a word that's been around in English since the 14th century, stemming from the Latin word *succedere*, meaning either "to succeed" or "to take the place of," depending on its use.
- **"Secession" is a breaking away or departure from something**, with examples including the secession of many southern states from the United States during the U.S. Civil War, the many independent countries that broke off from the U.S.S.R., and the interest of the Basque regions to separate from the rest of Spain. The first use of this word in English was in the early 17th century, where it arrived after a long journey that began with the Latin word *secedere*, meaning "to rebel" or "to withdraw."
- "Success," of course, is a victory of sorts—though the nature of success, I'll always argue, is up to you. Its root is the same Latin word that gives us "succession," which I find quite optimistic. Way to have some faith in your leadership, English language.

Thinking on the use of these words: Perhaps if some don't like the succession order of leadership, they could plan a secession of their group from the whole organization. Will they find success with this? Only time will tell.

We don't have much hope for seceding from the English language in our everyday life, so take one more moment with this, folks. Will you succeed with it? I have no doubt.

What Do You Call Your Story?

Memoirs, autobiographies, multi-generational epics, and beyond, there are a lot of categories a family story can fall into. Is this worth stressing over? Not at all. But if you're planning on taking the ideas gathered within this workbook into a larger project, let's chat genres. You're curious, and there are simple answers.

What is an autobiography?

AN AUTOBIOGRAPHY IS a story of your own life, or more generally a story where the author is describing their own life journey. It does not need to be chronological, but it can catalogue moments and events without any specific theme or narrative structure, which are characteristics more common in a memoir.

What is a memoir?

A MEMOIR, THOUGH SIMILAR, is not an autobiography. Instead of capturing your own full life story, a memoir captures a chapter or a specific theme about your life, with a narrative focused around a singular goal, quest, or problem. It is not a cataloging of facts and moments in your life but one piece of your life story—perhaps focused on something essential that changed or defined who you are, or something about your life that gives a unique perspective that the world hasn't frequently encountered.

What is a biography?

A BIOGRAPHY IS SIMILAR to an autobiography; however, the subject is not the writer themselves. The author is capturing someone else's life story. Perhaps in the case of a project that might come out of this workbook, a biography might be the story you write about an ancestor and the impact that this individual had on the world—or maybe just your world.

What is narrative nonfiction?

NONFICTION IS BOUND by the truth; whereas fiction is bound only by the limits of the imagination. Nonfiction can come in many forms, but narrative nonfiction is shaped around storytelling—around the telling of the narrative rather than purely the capturing of the true facts.

For example, a history or science textbook is nonfiction. There may not necessarily be stories told there, but rather a collection of well-explained factual information. Biographies, autobiographies, and memoirs are commonly written as narrative nonfiction, with the voice of a storyteller leading the way rather than an academic presenting an arrangement of facts. These sub-genres of nonfiction tell stories, often taking on a structure not so different from a novel, yet—of course—their material is true.

DOES EVERYONE EMBARKING upon the journey of this workbook need to define where they are headed? Not at all. Sometimes, writers just write without a destination, and that is fine too. And does everyone need to record their family history and stick only to the historical truth? Well, you could argue that family tall-tales, hyperboles, and folklore can play into the core of a family as much as anything else. These are all decisions for you, writer. Stepping beyond the nonfiction space and into fiction inspired by true stories is well within the possibilities. Anything is within your creative grasp if you choose for it to be. Here, we've simply started with what you know to be true. What comes next is up to you.

Keep Sharing

Every single day of our lives, we are surrounded by stories, stories that empower us or devastate us, stories true, stories manipulated, and stories that are absolute fabrications. It's true now, and it has been as long as there have been listeners captivated by a good tale. And you can claim your stories. Capture every piece of them, from the moments of fear to the moments of awakening to the moments that drive you to action to the moments that send you back to your family and friends, hugging them tighter than ever.

Eleanor Roosevelt, Frederick Douglass, Anne Frank ... so many before us have told their stories and changed the world. All of our stories might not be destined for the history books, but that doesn't mean that we don't have tales to tell that define us and the generations that follow us. It's your turn. What you do with your stories is up to you, but collecting them is an essential project.

To all those who have always wanted to write it down, here's your moment. Seize the opportunity. If not now, when? And then keep the tradition going. Storytelling is how we understand who we are, who we've been, and who we can become. It's humanity at our simplest and yet our finest. Keep sharing your stories. Keep listening to the stories of others, seeking out the true stories amidst all the noise. It's in little ways like this that we can empower the world. And who wouldn't want to be a part of that?

Author's Note

I have been fascinated by the English language and the power of stories ever since I can remember. Thinking back to the earliest of written storytellers, from Herodotus in ancient Greece to Sima Qian in ancient China, I am a bit in awe of the breakthrough moments when oral traditions and simple record-keeping transformed into narratives captured in written words for the world and the future to remember. Yet storytelling isn't just for the ground-breaking revolutionaries of the written word. It's for all of us.

There's power in well-composed communications and well-told stories. This power is what I sought to harness in my first two books, *Get a Grip on Your Grammar: 250 Writing and Editing Reminders for the Curious or Confused* (Career Press, 2017) and *The Novel Editing Workbook: 105 Tricks & Tips for Revising your Fiction Manuscript* (Davro Press, 2020). I'm so proud to add *The Family Story Workbook* to my collection, because we are indeed all writers and storytellers—every single one of us, in whatever shape that may take in our lives.

FOR THOSE INTERESTED in learning more about storytelling and the fascinating intricacies of the English language, I invite you to sign up for my monthly language tips and trivia newsletter at **Kris-Spisak.com**.

Happy writing, all!

Acknowledgments

Thank you to my readers and my writing community. Without your encouragement, this project idea may have never moved from a twinkle in my eye to a fleshed out full workbook project. You expressed your interest and encouraged me to keep going after I played with some of these ideas via social media and video prompts early on, and you reaffirmed how important certain stories can be.

Thank you to my family, who were not only guinea pigs with my early questions but who also lovingly pushed me to go deeper and always deeper. Thank you for the endless support and assistance, Lee Hawkins, Katharine Herndon, Karen A. Chase, Leslie Saunderlin, Lisa Hagan, and Frank Petroski. You all empower my goals and creativity in so many ways.

I am so appreciative of the storytellers—whether sharing tales through spoken, written, danced, drawn, or countless other forms. You all empower us to see our world more clearly than ever, and we should all be endlessly grateful for that.

Also by Kris Spisak

Get a Grip on Your Grammar: 250 Writing and Editing Reminders for the Curious or Confused (Career Press, 2017)

"Is it a dash or a colon here? Should I write first person or third? Is it 'already' or 'all ready'? In this handy manual, grammar guru Kris Spisak offers us her thoughts and tips on the writing questions that dog every writer's life. You'll want to keep a copy on your desk."

– *Meg Medina, Newbery and Pura Belpré Award-winning Author*

"I know about as much about grammar as I do about kite surfing, but Kris Spisak's delightful, breezy take has dark powers that give a rookie like me fingers instead of left thumbs, light instead of fog."

– *Kevin Smokler, Author of* Brat Pack America: A Love Letter to 80s Teen Movies *(Rare Bird Books, 2016)*

Available wherever books are sold.

The Novel Editing Workbook: 105 Tricks & Tips for Revising Your Fiction Manuscript (Davro Press, 2020)

"A must-have workbook for anyone ready to write a novel or about to edit one. Kris Spisak's first-person approach makes readers feel as though they have a writing coach looking over their shoulders."

– Ann Marie Sabath, "Book Whisperer";
Author of Everybody Has A Book In Them: How To Bring It Out

"This is the second time Kris has written a book that's helped my career. She asks the hard questions that authors need on the path from idea to publication, while respecting your unique method of thinking and writing. Kris understands that writing is work, but it doesn't have to be a disorganized grind—and this book gave me a framework I could use to edit faster, more accurately, and in ways I hadn't considered."

– Terry Maggert, Author of thirty-two novels

"When you're staring at a messy mountain of your own prose, Kris Spisak is the kind, wide-eyed mountaineer handing you a hiking stick, water bottle, and map. Keep *The Novel Editing Workbook* on your desk as a guide through the wilds and you'll come out with a polished novel on the other side."

– Lee Savino, USA Today Bestselling Romance Author

Available wherever books are sold.

www.ingramcontent.com/pod-product-compliance
Lightning Source LLC
Chambersburg PA
CBHW071233080526
44587CB00013BA/1592